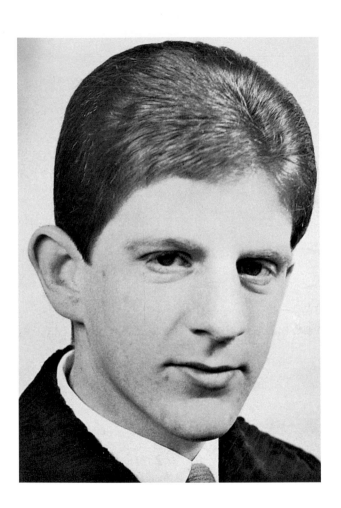

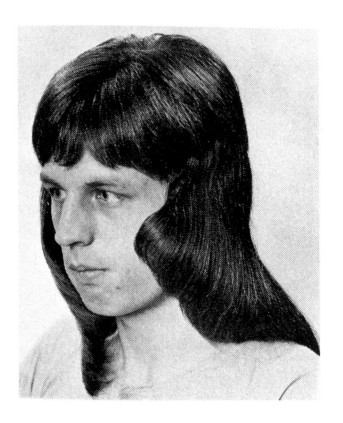

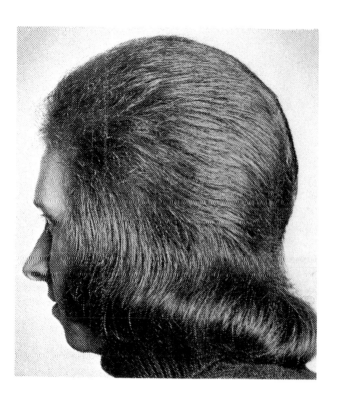

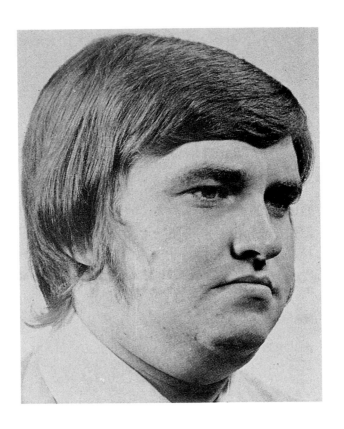

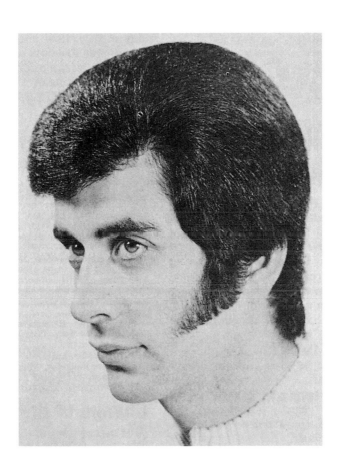

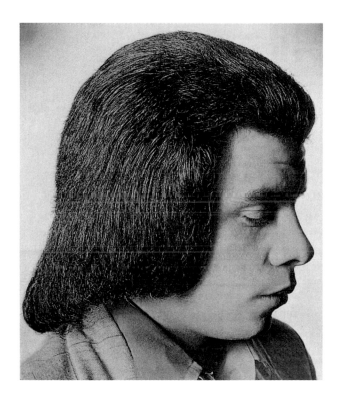

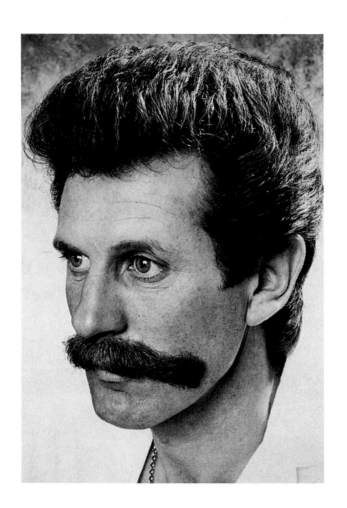

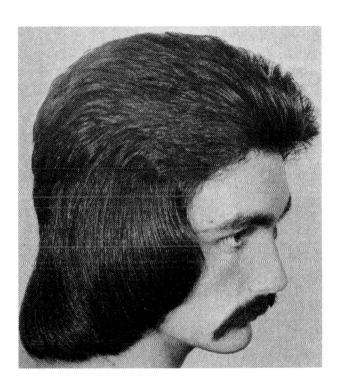

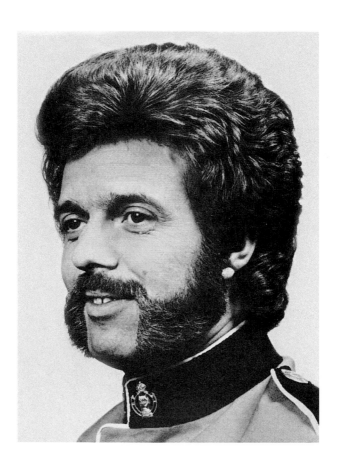

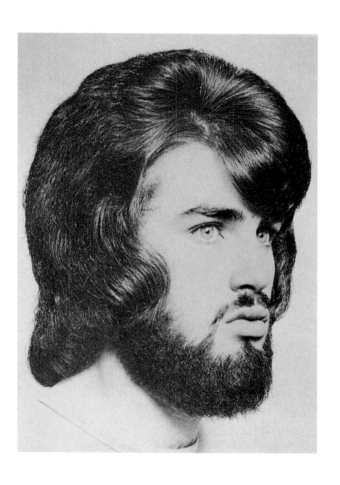

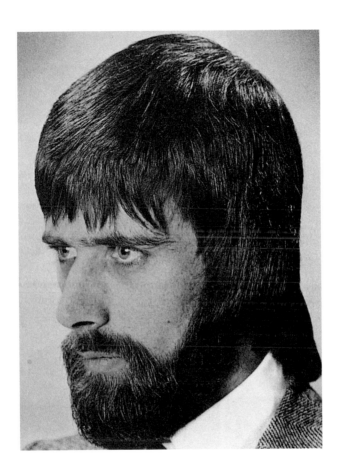

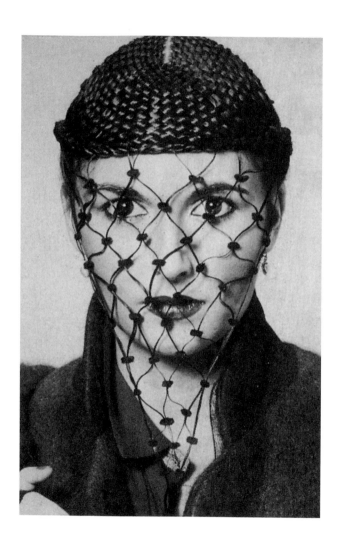

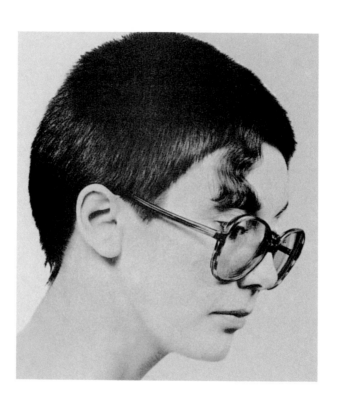

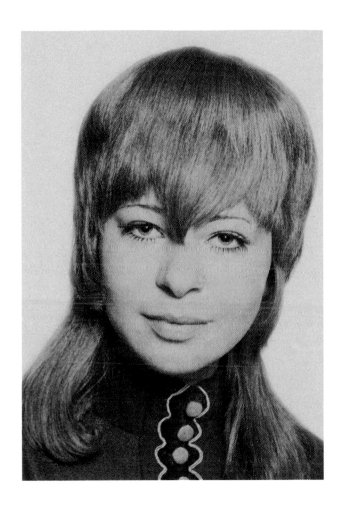

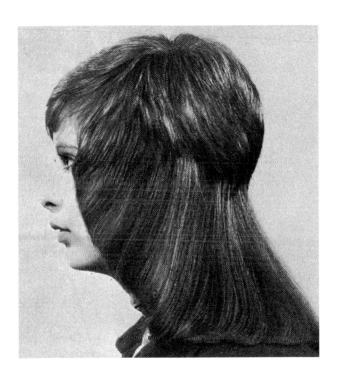

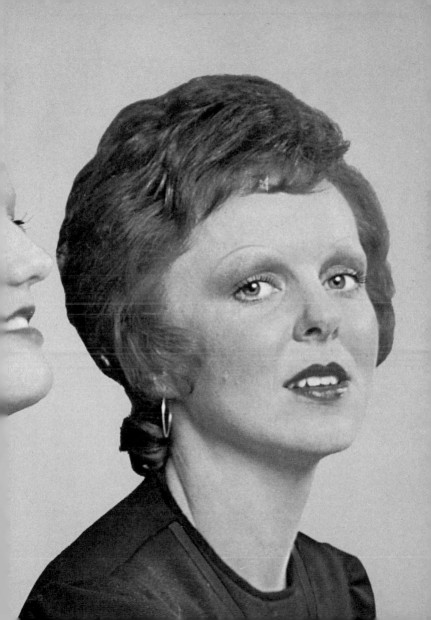

TO OUR PARENTS

FIRST PUBLISHED IN GREAT BRITAIN 2002

THIS COLLECTION COPYRIGHT © 2002 BY JAMES INNES-SMITH

BLOOMSBURY PUBLISHING PLC,
38 SOHO SQUARE, LONDON W1D 3HB

THE MORAL RIGHT OF THE AUTHOR HAS BEEN ASSERTED
A CIP CATALOGUE RECORD FOR THIS BOOK IS AVAILABLE
FROM THE BRITISH LIBRARY

ISBN 0 7475 6013 7

10 9 8 7 6 5 4 3

PRINTED IN CHINA BY C&C OFFSET PRINTING CO., LTD

BAD HAIR
BY JAMES INNES-SMITH
AND HENRIETTA WEBB

DESIGNED BY NATHAN BURTON

WITH SPECIAL THANKS TO JOHN SNETT: VASOS, GRAPE
STREET; VINCENZO, MARYLEBONE HIGH STREET; NEW LOOK,
BETHNAL GREEN ROAD, MARIO, CHILTERN STREET; ANDREW
CHRISTOFI AT ANDREW LAWRENCE; MATHEW AND SON,
SHEPHERDS BUSH; HAIRDRESSERS JOURNAL; THE LONDON
COLLEGE OF FASHION.

CREDITS: P26, HAIR BY CLIP JOINT, LONDON (HAIRDRESSERS
JOURNAL, SEPTEMBER 1972); P50, HAIR BY CHRIS CHAPMAN,
NORWICH, NORFOLK; P74, HAIR BY RAYMOND AT MANELINE,
PHOTOGRAPHY BY DAVID GLEW (HAIRDRESSERS JOURNAL,
AUGUST 1971); P87, HAIR BY RICCI BURNS (HAIRDRESSERS
JOURNAL, OCTOBER 1970); P95, HAIR BY MICHAELJOHN,
LONDON; P96, HAIR BY TONI AND GUY; P104, HAIR BY JASON
BRANDLER ATJINGLES INTERNATIONAL (HAIRDRESSERS
JOURNAL, DECEMBER 1980).